COLOUR BY NUMBERS

# PATTERNS
## FROM
# NATURE

# COLOUR BY NUMBERS

# PATTERNS
## FROM
# NATURE

### 45 BEAUTIFUL DESIGNS FOR STRESS REDUCTION

Glyn Bridgewater

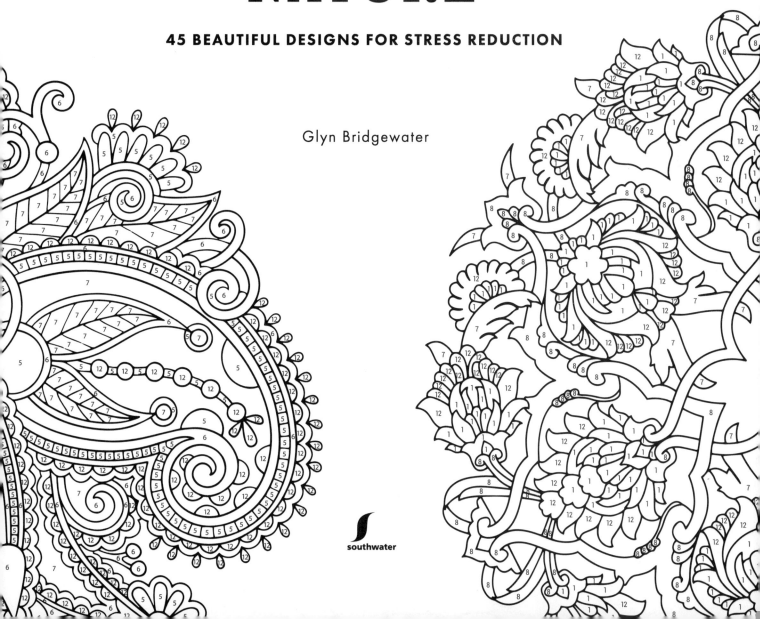

southwater

# Introduction

Take a peek inside this beautiful book, where you and your pencils are the last pieces of the puzzle...

Modern life can at times be stressful for all of us, from exams and commuting to digital distractions. It's no coincidence that people are turning to colouring books as a way of escaping hectic day-to-day tasks for a brief time, and focusing on a creative activity that is entirely in the present. Colouring-in is a form of mindful meditation, where anxieties can be relieved by the simple act of picking up some pencils and enjoying the relaxing process of filling in the blanks.

In this colour-by-numbers book the illustrations have been separated into segments marked with a number. Each number corresponds to one of 12 colours on a palette from crimson red and bright orange through calming greens and cool blues to rich purple and dazzling pink. You will find this palette printed on the cover. Simply fold the flap onto the opposite page you are working on to have a handy reference while completing your picture. With the shades already chosen, it is simply up to you to complete the transformation from black and white outline to vivid displays of bright colour. Any small areas with no number are intended to remain white. As you slowly build up the design you will feel immense satisfaction at finishing the puzzle and bringing these wonderful artworks to life. The same picture is repeated without numbers on the left-hand page for you to complete using a colour palette entirely of your own choosing.

The enchanting pictures and patterns inside these pages are all inspired by natural themes. You will find summery meadows and secret woodlands, and evocative depictions of life under the sea. A deer gets lost among the overgrown flowers, while fishes swim together through the coral. Roses spring out from the turf while exotic plants sway in the breeze. The colourings take the pictures to new realms with fantastic new combinations of tone and shade. Abstract patterns based on natural shapes create beautiful kaleidoscopes of colour. Young and old alike will relish the joy of discovery in bringing these nature scenes to their full vibrant potential. Ten minutes each day will be enough to feel the therapeutic benefits – but you may find yourself drawn in for hours!

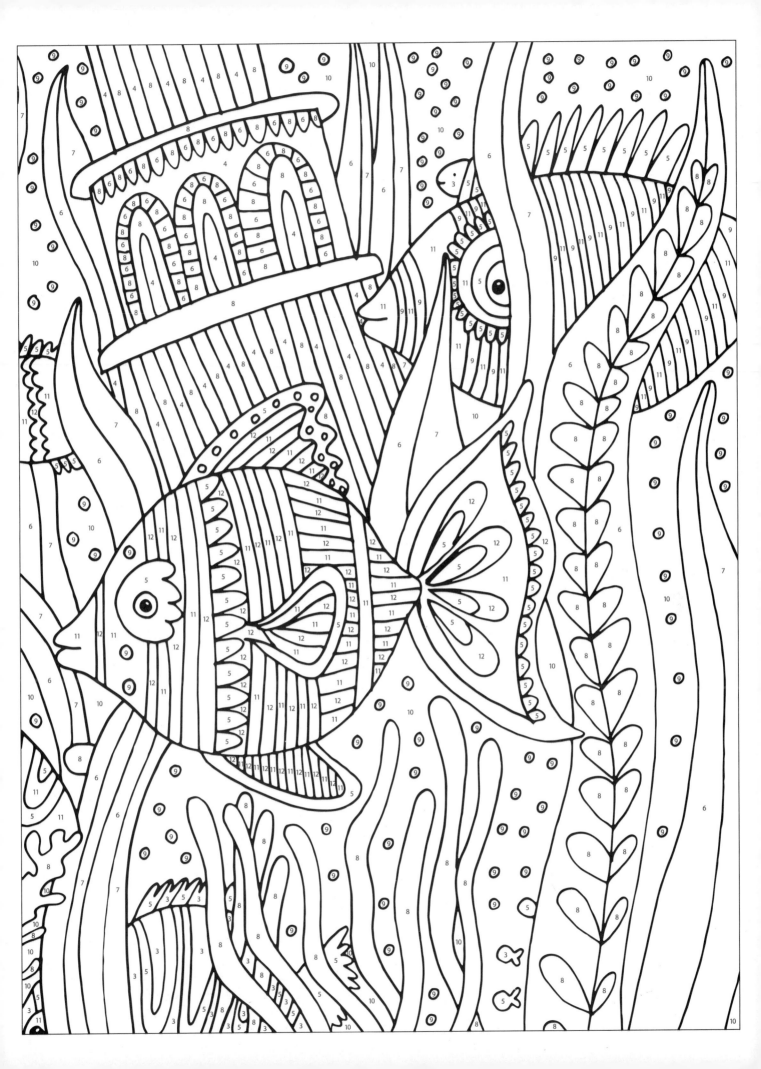

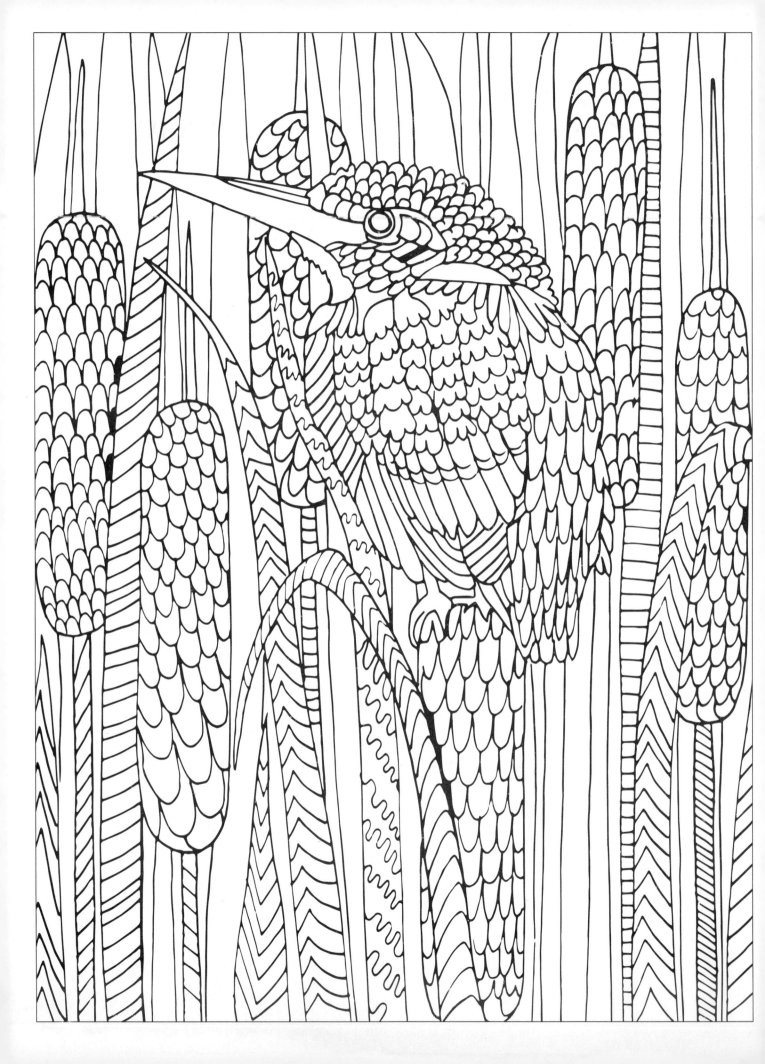

This edition published by Southwater, an imprint of Anness Publishing Limited

108 Great Russell Street, London WC1B 3NA

info@anness.com; www.annesspublishing.com

twitter @Anness_Books

Publisher: Joanna Lorenz

Editorial Director: Helen Sudell

Designer: Glyn Bridgewater

Production Director: Ben Worley

Illustrations: Shutterstock

Publisher's Note

Although the information in this book is believed to be acccurate at the time of going to press neither
the author nor the publisher can accept any legal responsibility or liability for any errors or omissions
that may have been made.